Li

Ancient

Egypt

A Journey into the Mysterious Past

Denise Doxey, Ph.D.

RUNNING PRESS

PHILADELPHIA · LONDON

A NOTE TO PARENTS:

This interactive, educational kit is designed to teach and entertain children, but it contains small parts which could cause injury if swallowed. This kit should not be used by children under six years of age without adult supervision. Please read the complete instructions inside before using this kit.

—*Running Press Book Publishers*

© 1996 by Running Press

Printed in Canada

Discovery Kit is a trademark of Running Press Book Publishers

9 8 7 6 5 4 3 2 1
Digit on the right indicates the number of this printing

Library of Congress Cataloging-in-Publication Number 96-68398
ISBN 1-56138-750-9

Package and book cover design by Diane Miljat
Book interior design by Frances J. Soo Ping Chow
Picture research by Susan Oyama
Edited by Elaine M. Bucher
The text was set in Goudy and Goudy Handtooled
Package front and back photograph (Tut): Erich Lessing/Art Resource, NY
Package front photograph (children): Stephen Mullen
Package interior photographs: Stephen Mullen
Book front cover photograph (Tut): Erich Lessing/Art Resource, NY
Book front and back cover photograph (pyramids): Jim Graham/GSI
Book interior illustrations: Helen Driggs
Book interior photographs: Foto Marburg/Art Resource, NY: pp. 21, 22. Erich Lessing/Art Resource, NY: p. 35. Courtesy of the Library of Congress Photoduplication Service: p. 62 (HABS 605694). University of Pennsylvania Museum, Philadelphia: p. 25 (Neg. #S4-141977), p. 26 (Neg. #S4-141979), p. 27 (Neg. #S4-133264), p. 28 (Neg. #S8-31388), p. 32 (Neg. #G8-31231), p. 36 (Neg. #S4-141443), p. 37 (Neg. #S4-141436), p. 39 (Neg. #S4-141437), p. 41 (Neg. #S4-141978), p. 43 (Neg. #S4-141976), p. 49 (Neg. #S4-38010), p. 50 (Neg. #S4-139317), p. 61 (Neg. #S8-21366). © Denise Doxey: pp. 15, 17, 29, 60.

This kit containing this book may be ordered by mail from the publisher.
Please add $2.50 for postage and handling.
But try your bookstore first!

Running Press Book Publishers
125 South Twenty-second Street
Philadelphia, Pennsylvania 19103-4399

Contents

Part One:
Who Were the Ancient Egyptians?

Egyptian Stories of Creation

Before the beginning of time, all that existed was a dark, empty, and frightening body of water called Nun. As this body of water receded, a mound of dry land emerged. Upon this mound was the god Atum. Atum created Shu and Tefnut, the air god and the moisture goddess. Shu and Tefnut then became the parents of Geb, the earth god, and Nut, the sky goddess, whose body was covered with stars. Shu stood, lifting his daughter so that air filled the space between the earth and the sky. Geb and Nut had four children, the gods Osiris and Seth and the goddesses Isis and Nephthys. All other gods and goddesses, and eventually humans as well, are descendants of these nine gods. Among the most important of these descendants was Ra, the god of the sun, who sometimes took the form of a great falcon or a man with a falcon's head.

This story, the best-known Egyptian myth of creation, originated in the city of Iunu [YOU-new] (later called Heliopolis by the Greeks). In other parts of Egypt different versions of the tale were found. For example, in the city of Memphis, the local god Ptah was said to be the original god and to have created Atum and the other gods simply by uttering their names. At Khemunu [Kem-OO-new] (later called

Hermopolis by the Greeks) Thoth, the god of wisdom, writing, and

ATUM

SHU
air god

TEFNUT
moisture goddess

GEB
earth god

NUT
sky goddess

OSIRIS   **SETH**   **ISIS**   **NEPTHYS**

the moon, was originally believed to be the creator of the gods and humanity. In one variation of this story Thoth set forth an egg from which the other gods hatched. In another the gods emerged from a lotus flower floating on the waters of Nun. All these variations may seem a bit confusing to the modern reader, and there is evidence that they sometimes confused even the ancient Egyptians themselves! But within them all is the same basic theme—a safe, habitable world emerges from a watery darkness and is populated first by gods and finally by men and women.

The "Two Lands" of Egypt

In order to understand how the ancient Egyptians lived and thought, we need to understand the unique landscape of Egypt itself. The most significant feature of the landscape is the Nile river. Egypt is located at the northeast corner of Africa, in a region largely made up of deserts. The Nile river is fed by a series of rivers, including the Blue Nile and the White Nile, flowing northward from the highlands of Ethiopia. Heavy summer rains in the African highlands cause the Nile to reach its highest point late in the summer and to overflow its banks throughout the entire length of Egypt during August and September. These floods water the fields and deposit a fresh layer of

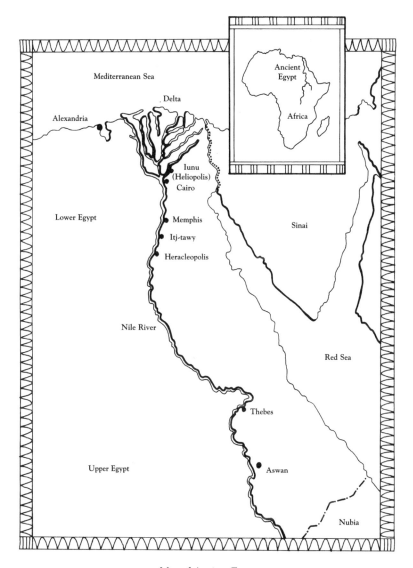

Map of Ancient Egypt

fertile soil each year. The receding flood waters, from which mounds of dry land gradually appear, probably inspired Egyptian stories of creation.

The ancient Egyptians planted their crops in the fall and harvested them in the winter and spring. When the river valley was not flooded, various systems of irrigation were used to bring water from the river to the fields. Throughout the southern and central parts of Egypt the Nile provided a long strip of very fertile land in the midst of a desert. The Egyptians called their land *Kemet* [KEM-et] (meaning "Black Land") and, equating Egypt with the Nile river valley, used the same name for the valley itself. The desert was named *Deshret* [DESH-ret] (meaning "Red Land"). In contrast to the fertile valley, the desert was a land where the harsh climate, wild animals, and "uncivilized" foreign peoples could all pose a threat to anyone who ventured into it.

In the northern part of Egypt, where the Nile river flows into the Mediterranean Sea, the river valley gives way to the delta. Here the river itself separates into a number of channels, and the fertile land spreads out like a fan. In ancient Egypt there was a much greater amount of well-watered land in the delta, although in many areas it was too wet and swampy for agriculture. Among the crops grown in the delta was papyrus [pa-PIE-rus], used to make an early form of paper.

The ancient Egyptians themselves seem to have realized the distinct characteristics of the valley and the delta from a very early date. The delta, although it is to the north, was (and still is) known as Lower Egypt because the height of the land is lower than that in the valley. The valley was known as Upper Egypt. According to Egyptian myth, a legendary king from Upper Egypt named Menes conquered Lower Egypt to unite the "two lands" and form a single nation. The pharaoh [FAIR-o] was therefore known as the "Lord of the Two Lands." For much of Egyptian history the capital city was Memphis, located near the point at which Upper and Lower Egypt meet. The modern capital, Cairo [KI-ro], is in a similar location today.

For purposes of government the Nile valley and delta were divided into districts, twenty-two in Upper Egypt and twenty in Lower Egypt. The Egyptian word for a district was *sepat* [SEE-pot], but today historians often use the ancient Greek word *nome* [rhymes with "home"]. Although there were a few fairly large cities, most people lived in small towns or villages surrounded by agricultural land. Each town had its own cemetery and its own local god or goddess with his or her own temple and priesthood. Because many Egyptian towns were located in the river valley and are now buried under modern villages and deep layers of soil, archaeologists working in Egypt have historically learned more about the temples and tombs than the homes of the living. This situation, however, has changed with improved excavation techniques, and our picture of life in the villages is gradually becoming much clearer.

An Egyptian Family

Because so much of what has been preserved from ancient Egypt comes from royal monuments, tombs, and temples, we know a lot more about the activities of the pharaohs than about those of everyday people. However, we can learn quite a bit about the lives of wealthy people from the scenes painted in their tombs and from personal letters that have survived to the present day.

Since horses were quite valuable, Egyptian farmers never used them in the fields. Instead, they used cattle or even men to pull their plows.

Egyptologists have discovered an important group of letters written by a well-to-do farmer and priest named Hekanakht [HECK-a-nocked] that have provided much-needed information about the lives of the ancient Egyptians. Egyptologists speculate that Hekanakht lived around 2000 B.C., when the Nile river was lower than normal and food was scarce. The letters were written from Hekanakht to his family while he was away from home on business in southern Egypt. They show that Hekanakht was very strict and somewhat miserly, repeatedly warning his son to work hard, watch his spending, and look after his younger brothers. The women in the house are also mentioned, and Hekanakht fires a housemaid who has not been getting along with his new wife. He also addresses a letter to his mother, to whom he speaks respectfully about the family business and finances.

Hekanakht's household included himself and his new wife, at least five sons, apparently from an earlier marriage, Hekanakht's mother and another female relative named Hetep, and several household servants, including a hairdresser. In addition, seasonal workers were paid in food to assist with the sowing and harvesting of crops. Hekanakht rented the land on which he farmed, growing mainly cereal grains such as wheat, barley, and emmer. Since money was not used in ancient Egypt at this time, the family paid the rent in cloth, which was woven by the women.

They owned some cattle, using the bulls for sowing crops just as people are shown doing on the walls of contemporary tombs. Grain and other food was given out to each member of the household, and Hekanakht insisted that they be fed only so long as they were working hard!

Activity: *Make Your Own Egyptian Tunic*

S everal types of garments were worn by the ancient Egyptians. Fashions for men and women changed significantly over time. During the summer months tunics were made out of lightweight linen, while during the winter they were fashioned from heavier (and warmer) wool. With a few objects from around the house, you can learn how to make a tunic that was popular around 1500 B.C.

First, find an old bed sheet or another large piece of fabric; it should be at least four feet wide and twice the length of your body from your shoulders to your knees. You will need to cut the fabric, so check with your parents to make sure that the fabric you have is okay to use. You will also need a long strip of cloth or a wide scarf (about two feet wide) to use as a sash, and a pair of scissors.

Fold the fabric in half and hold it up in front of you. Folded, it should be long enough to hang down to your knees, but it can reach as far as your ankles if you prefer.

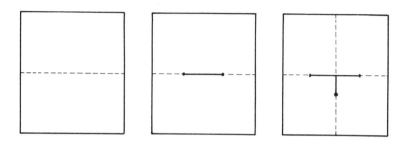

You will need to cut a hole for your head in the center of the fabric. You may want to ask one of your parents or another adult to help you do this. Begin by drawing a line just under a foot long, as shown. Cut along the line. In the center of your line, make a six-inch-long cut at a right angle to the first.

Then drape the cloth over your head and stand with your arms sticking straight out to your sides. Adjust the tunic (or have someone

else adjust it) so that it hangs down straight. If the sides of the tunic reach out past your hands, you should trim the cloth.

Now take the strip of fabric or scarf and wrap it around your waist like a sash, as shown. With your sash tied and a pair of sandals on your feet, you're ready to sail the Nile with the ancient Egyptians!

Timeline of Ancient Egyptian Civilization

One of the truly outstanding features of ancient Egyptian civilization is the length of time it lasted. The unification of the country into a single kingdom, along with the earliest use of written records and the beginning of the reign of the first pharaoh, took place about 3000 B.C. Although many important changes took place, the basic features of the government, language, and society remained in place for more than three thousand years. By the time the famous queen Cleopatra was born, the great pyramid of King Khufu was already as ancient to her as she is to us today!

Since ancient times, historians have organized the pharaohs of ancient Egypt into groups of kings belonging to the same family line. These groups, known as *dynasties*, are in turn organized into larger periods. The period before which Egypt was unified under a single king is known as the *Predynastic Period*. The *Early Dynastic Period* includes the first three dynasties, from about 2920 to 2575 B.C. During this time, the art, architecture, and government of Egypt developed into the form that would later be recognized as typically Egyptian. Egypt also began to expand its boundaries, conquering much of Nubia to its south.

The fourth, fifth, and sixth dynasties make up the *Old Kingdom*, which lasted from about 2575 to 2135 B.C. For the most part, it was a period of strong royal power during which Egyptian armies continued to campaign in the north and east. Trade also flourished in both directions. This was the greatest period of pyramid building in Egyptian

The fourth dynasty was the greatest period of pyramid building
in Egyptian history. During this period, the Great Pyramids
and the famous Sphinx at Giza were built.

history, the most impressive examples of which are the fourth dynasty pyramids at Giza, where the famous Sphinx also stands.

Toward the end of the sixth dynasty, royal power deteriorated and the government eventually collapsed. A series of poor floods may have caused a famine that contributed to the decline. The period that followed, from around 2134 to 2040 B.C., is known as the *First Intermediate Period* and includes the seventh through tenth dynasties as well as the beginning of the eleventh. Throughout this period, rival kings and their families competed for power, and the unity of Egypt was in jeopardy. Upper Egypt was ruled from the southern city of Thebes [THEEBS], while the government of Lower Egypt was centered at Heracleopolis [He-RACK-lee-OP-oh-lis].

During the eleventh dynasty, King Mentuhotep [MEN-too-HO-tep] II of Thebes reunited the country, signaling the beginning of the *Middle Kingdom*. The Middle Kingdom lasted from around 2040 to 1640 B.C. and included the end of the eleventh through the fourteenth dynasties. The first few kings ruled from Thebes, but in the twelfth dynasty a new capital was founded not far from Memphis and called Itj-tawy [Itch-TA-wee] (meaning "the one who seizes of the two lands").

Gradually the power of Egypt again declined, and the *Second Intermediate Period* began. During this period, which lasted from 1640 to

1550 B.C. and included the fifteenth through seventeenth dynasties, the delta was ruled by immigrants from the Middle East known today as the Hyksos [HICK-sos], a name derived from an Egyptian phrase meaning "rulers of foreign lands." In the south, Nubia regained its status as an influential rival, and foreign contacts led to innovations such as the horse and chariot, which had been unknown in Egypt up to this point.

Once again the move toward reunification came from Thebes. The pharaoh Ahmose [Ahm-OS-seh] drove the Hyksos from power and founded the eighteenth dynasty. The *New Kingdom*, made up of the eighteenth through twentieth dynasties, lasted from about 1550 to

Colossal statues of Ramesses II guard the temple he built at Abu Simbel.

1070 B.C. During this period, Egypt's foreign domination in both Nubia and the Near East reached its peak. Many of the most famous Egyptian kings, such as Thutmose [Thut-MO-seh] III of the eighteenth dynasty and Ramesses [RAM-zees] (also spelled Ramses or Rameses) II of the nineteenth, left records of great military campaigns. The kings ceased to be buried in pyramids and began cutting elaborate rock tombs in the cliffs to the west of Thebes. Many of Egypt's largest temples were built during this era, the most impressive being the great complex at Karnak dedicated to the Theban god Amun.

Although Egypt remained strong throughout the early twentieth dynasty, royal power once again disintegrated near the end of its reign, signaling the start of the *Third Intermediate Period* (c. 1070–712 B.C.). Egypt's power never again reached the height it had enjoyed during the New Kingdom, although there were periods of great prosperity. Egypt was again ruled by many different kings from different centers at the same time.

Throughout the *Late Period*, which lasted from about 712 to 332 B.C., Egypt was often ruled by foreigners. The Egyptian culture, however, remained intact. It was typical for these rulers, even when they were not Egyptian, to adopt the traditional titles, costumes, and even religious practices of the Egyptian pharaohs. During much of this period,

Egypt remained a key player in the political and military activities of the Middle East.

In 332 B.C., Alexander the Great of Macedonia conquered Egypt without a fight. Although Alexander showed a great deal of interest in Egypt, he died shortly after its conquest. During the next 250 years, Egypt was ruled by Greeks. This period is known as the *Ptolemaic* [TA-le-MAY-ic] *Period*, because most of the rulers were named Ptolemy. Although the kings were foreigners, Egypt remained an independent nation, and its major city, Alexandria, became one of the leading cultural centers of the Mediterranean world. Numerous Ptolemaic temples built for local Egyptian gods and goddesses remain standing in Egypt today. In 30 B.C., however, Roman forces defeated the last of the Ptolemaic rulers, the now famous queen Cleopatra, and Egypt was absorbed into the Roman Empire.

A Timeline of Major Events

c. 2920–2575 B.C.: The Early Dynastic Period

Dynasties 1, 2, and 3—*Khasekhemwy* (?–2649 B.C.)*
builds a funerary enclosure at Abydos. *Zoser*
(2630–2611 B.C.) builds the "Step Pyramid" at
Saqqara, the first monumental stone pyramid.

c. 2575–2135 B.C.: The Old Kingdom

Dynasties 4, 5, 6, and 7—The fourth dynasty pyramids at Giza, including the "Great Pyramid" and the
famous Sphinx, are built. *Snefru* (2575–2551 B.C.)
builds the "Bent Pyramid" and "Red Pyramid" at
Dahshur. *Unis* (2356–2323 B.C.) inscribes the oldest
preserved Egyptian religious text, the Pyramid Texts,
in his tomb.

2134–2040 B.C.: The First Intermediate Period

Dynasties 9 and 10—Kings rule from Heracleopolis
and Thebes.

*ALL DATES FOR PHARAOHS AND KINGS REFER TO THE PERIOD OF THEIR RULE.

2040–1640 B.C.: The Middle Kingdom

Dynasties 11, 12, and 13—*Mentuhotep II* (2061–2010 B.C.) defeats the Heracleopolitans and reunites Egypt. Some of the greatest works of Egyptian literature, including *The Story of Sinuhe* and *The Instruction of King Amenemhet*, are written.

1640–1550 B.C.: The Second Intermediate Period

Dynasties 14, 15, 16, and 17—Hyksos rulers from western Asia take power.

1550–1070 B.C.: The New Kingdom

Dynasties 18, 19, and 20—*Ahmose* (1550–1525 B.C.)

A New Kingdom Sphinx of the female "king" Hatshepsut

defeats the Hyksos and reunites Egypt. *Hatshepsut* (1473–1458 B.C.), a female "king," builds a funerary temple at Deir el Bahri, near Thebes, and erects obelisks at Karnak. In about 1348 B.C., *Amenhotep IV* (1353–1335 B.C.), also known as Akhenaten, prohibits worship of traditional gods. He and his wife, Nefertiti, move the capital to the new city of Akhenaten and introduce a new artistic style. Later, *Tutankhamun* (1333–1323 B.C.) restores the traditional gods and capital. He is the owner of the only intact royal tomb to survive until modern times. During his sixty-six year reign, *Ramesses II* (1290–1224 B.C.) leads an army against the Hittites and builds more surviving temples than any other pharaoh.

A limestone head of Amenhotep IV (Akhenaten)

1070–712 B.C.: The Third Intermediate Period

Dynasties 21, 22, 23, and 24—Kings rule from both Tanis and Sais.

712–332 B.C.: The Late Period

Dynasty 25, 26, 27, 28, 29, 30, and 31—Periods of independence alternate with invasions. Egypt is conquered by the Assrians and Persians during this period.

332–30 B.C.: The Ptolemaic Period

Alexander the Great (332–323 B.C.), a Macedonian Greek, conquers Egypt without a struggle and plans the building of Alexandria. Following Alexander's death, Ptolemy I (304–284 B.C.) becomes satrap of Egypt and declares himself an independent king. In 30 B.C., *Cleopatra VII*, the last Ptolemaic ruler, is defeated by the Romans, and Egypt is absorbed into the Roman Empire.

Part Two:

The Tomb and the Afterlife in Ancient Egypt

The Myth of Osiris

Accccording to Egyptian belief, Osiris [Oh-SY-ris] was the eldest son of Geb, the earth, and Nut, the sky. As the myth goes, Osiris introduced agriculture to the people of Egypt and was their king. Murdered by his ambitious younger brother Seth, Osiris's body was nailed in a chest and thrown into the Nile. Although the chest was carried out to sea, Osiris's wife, Isis [EYE-sis], found it and brought it back to Egypt. When Seth learned that the body had been returned, he dismembered the body and scattered its parts around the countryside. Upon discovering Seth's treachery, Isis gathered the pieces of her husband and, with the help of Anubis, the god of embalming, carefully mummified the pieces. Through her magical powers, Isis restored Osiris to life as the ruler of *Duat* [DEW-watt], the Egyptian underworld.

Osiris's only son, Horus, eventually attempted to regain his stolen inheritance from his uncle. A series of great battles between Horus and Seth followed. In one of these conflicts Seth gouged out Horus's eye, which was magically restored by the god Thoth. Thereafter, the eye of

Egyptian amulets from the Middle and New Kingdoms.
The amulets in the far-right row are udjat-eye amulets.

Horus (known as the *udjat-eye* [WA-jot]) became a powerful amulet. The bitter struggle between Horus and Seth lasted many years, until they finally brought their case before a court judged by nine of Egypt's most powerful gods. The gods, however, could not come to a decision, and the case dragged on for eighty years! Finally, Osiris sent a letter to each of the judges, threatening to send messengers from the afterlife to bring them into the world of the dead. Swayed by Osiris's threat, the court decided in favor of Horus and awarded him the throne of Egypt.

This myth appealed deeply to the ancient Egyptians, and they identified their living king with Horus. After his death, the king became one with Osiris and reigned in the underworld. Egyptian artists depicted Osiris as a human, usually with green skin (to represent his gift of farming), wrapped in mummy wrappings (because he was god of the dead), wearing the tall, feathered atef crown, and carrying the crook and flail (symbols of Egyptian kingship).

Preparing for an Egyptian Burial

All Egyptians hoped to join Osiris in the afterlife, a place filled with fields and waterways in which existence was very similar to life in Egypt. In order to do this, elaborate preparations were necessary. Egyptians who could afford to would begin preparing for their deaths while in the prime of life. First, a tomb was built or carved in rock and its walls decorated with a variety of scenes and texts, all of which had important symbolic functions.

When the time for burial came, the body was mummified in order to preserve it for the spirit in the afterlife. The process took seventy days to complete. The internal organs (the first part of the body to decay after death) were removed, wrapped separately, and carefully sealed in special jars. These jars, called *canopic*

LEFT: A bronze statuette of the Egyptian god of the dead, Osiris

jars, were placed in the tomb to be magically reunited with the body in the afterlife. If the person in question could afford a deluxe treatment, his or her brain was also removed. The brain was carefully extracted through the nostrils, a technique that was developed during the New Kingdom. Once the organs were removed, the body was packed in a powder called *natron* [NAY-tron], which absorbed the fluids and dried out the body. The dried corpse was then washed and wrapped in layers of linen bandages. Throughout the wrappings the Egyptians placed jewelry and an assortment of amulets, each with an important magical function in the afterlife.

While this procedure was under way, burial offerings were assembled for use in the next world. The gifts included objects used by the dead person during his or her life and items made especially for the burial. In a very rich tomb, the offerings might include numerous vases and jars made of stone and pottery, pieces of furniture, weapons, tools, board games, jewelry, clothing, cosmetic items, musical instruments, and toys. The burial offerings of a common person would likely include only a few necessities and objects of senti-mental or ritual value. Meals were also necessary in the afterlife, so food

ABOVE RIGHT: **The mummy of an Egyptian child**

and beverages were placed in the tomb. Along with actual food, pictures of food and menu lists were thought to provide food magically in the afterlife.

On the day of burial the body was brought to the tomb on a sledge accompanied by a large procession. In the procession were the family, professional mourners, funerary priests, officials, and servants carrying the offerings. Priests burned incense and anointed the ground with milk. In front of the tomb ritual dancers performed and a priest read the necessary religious spells. Next came a ceremony known as the "Opening of the Mouth." The mouth of the mummy case was touched with a series of tools and amulets to restore speech, sight, and hearing to the deceased. A funerary feast then took place at the tomb, and the body was placed in the burial chamber. Finally, when everyone had left, a priest swept away the footprints with a small broom.

The burial rites did not end here, however. The family had to provide a continuous supply of food, drink, and other offerings. Professional mortuary priests could also perform this function, and some wealthy officials drew up

The limestone sarcophagus of a Late Period Egyptian priest

detailed legal contracts arranging for their care after death. In addition, the Egyptians believed that the dead could continue to interfere, either for good or bad, in the lives of the living. Therefore, they used offerings, prayers, and even letters written to the dead to make sure that their relatives were happy.

An 18th-dynasty tomb mural in the Valley of the Kings

Royal and Private Tombs

Egyptian tombs could vary greatly in type, depending upon the time period in which they were built and the status of their owners. Wealthy officials, and especially kings, took great care to make their tombs impressive and to protect the offerings inside from tomb robbers. They were also careful to include scenes and texts specifically designed to help them reach the afterlife.

In the Old and Middle Kingdoms, kings were buried inside pyramids. Within the solid stone (and later mud-brick) were elaborately designed ramps and chambers housing the king's body and burial goods. At the base of each pyramid stood the funerary temple, in which the offertory rituals could be carried out once the pyramid itself was permanently sealed. Since the pyramids were usually built in the desert, a causeway connected the funerary temple to the valley temple, located along the edge of the cultivated land. From the fifth dynasty onward, the interior walls of the burial chamber and other chambers were inscribed with religious texts and magical spells known as the Pyramid Texts, which were designed to assist the king on his difficult route to the afterlife and to help him when the time came to be judged by Osiris.

In the early New Kingdom, a major change occurred. Rather than building pyramids, the kings began carving tombs in the rock cliffs to the west of Thebes in a valley known today as the Valley of the Kings. A nearby valley known as the Valley of the Queens served as the location for the tombs of queens and royal children. Separate mortuary temples, often huge and very elaborate, were built near the cultivated land. By this time the Pyramid Texts had evolved into a new form, the *Book of the Dead,* which was painted on the walls of royal tombs. By the nineteenth dynasty, the Egyptians were adding large and beautifully colored figures of the king surrounded by gods and goddesses to the tomb walls.

Elite private citizens who lived in the area around Memphis were buried beneath large, flat-topped, rectangular structures built of mud brick. These tombs are known as *mastabas* [mas-TAH-bahs]. Inside the solid mud-brick structure was an offering chapel or series of chapels. The walls of these chapels, as well as parts of the exterior of the mastaba, were lined with stone blocks and decorated with carved and painted illustrations and inscriptions. The most important feature of the chapel was the false door, a stone slab carved to represent a doorway and inscribed with offering prayers. The Egyptians believed that the spirit of the deceased could pass through the door, and they left offerings for the spirit in front of it. A second important feature was the *serdab* [SAIR-dab], a sealed chamber in which a statue of the dead person stood. This statue could serve as a substitute for the actual mummy when the spirit returned to the tomb and needed a body to inhabit. Although the serdab was sealed off, a slit in the wall of the chapel allowed the statue to "see" out.

This stone slab from a 6th-dynasty Egyptian mastaba was carved
to represent a doorway and inscribed with offering prayers.

In southern Egypt, where the Nile valley was narrower, nobles had their tombs cut into the rocky cliffs just as the kings did during the New Kingdom. These officials often had pictures of themselves or inscriptions describing their virtues and the highlights of their careers carved around the front doorway of their tomb. Inside, there was an outer chapel often decorated with scenes of daily life and rituals connected with the tomb and an inner shrine devoted strictly to the afterlife. As in mastabas, a false door and a statue of the deceased were standard features of the rock-cut tombs. The bodies were actually buried in shafts cut into the floor.

Activity: *Decorate your own "tomb walls"*

For thousands of years, Egyptian officials decorated their tomb walls with specific types of scenes arranged in a particular way. They began planning these scenes while they were still in the prime of life. With a bit of imagination, you can design what your own tomb walls might have looked like if you had lived in ancient Egypt.

You will need a large piece of paper, a pencil, a ruler, and crayons, colored pencils, or magic markers.

Using your ruler, divide about two-thirds of the paper into four or five horizontal rows as shown. The rest of the page should be left open.

```
_____

_____        Draw
                               Yourself
_____          Here

_____
```

One common subject of tomb walls was daily life, or rather the sort of ideal life that the Egyptians hoped to live in the afterlife. To create this type of tomb wall, draw a picture of yourself in the open space standing and facing the rest of the page. Above the picture, write a short description of yourself, listing your best qualities. Then, in the horizontal rows, draw pictures of your friends, family, neighbors, and classmates doing the sorts of things you see them doing every day. You might also include your pet if you have one. The Egyptians often showed their favorite dog or cat seated beside them inside their tombs.

Another typical scene in an Egyptian tomb showed offerings being brought to the funeral feast. Divide the paper just as you did for the daily life scene, but leave a little wider space for the picture of yourself. This time, draw yourself sitting at a table with some of your favorite foods on it. Above your picture, list the types of foods you would like to eat forever in the afterlife. In the rows, draw pictures of your family and friends bringing your favorite foods, games, clothing, and other possessions.

The Egyptians usually labeled the people they showed in their tombs, and you might want to do the same. Beside each person in your pictures, include a caption telling who they are.

The Discovery of Tutankhamun's Tomb

King Tutankhamun [TOOT-onk-ah-mun], better known to the world today as "King Tut," became pharaoh when he was only about nine years old and died before he reached the age of twenty. He lived at the end of the Eighteenth Dynasty, ruling from around 1333 to 1323 B.C. Partly because of his age and the short length of his reign, he did not leave as many monuments as the other kings of his dynasty. Earlier members of his family, notably the famous king Akhenaten [Ahk-ah-NOT-en] and his wife, Nefertiti [Nef-er-TEET-ee], had held revolutionary religious beliefs and had forsaken the many gods of Egypt. Although Tutankhamun returned to the old religion,

This golden mask was discovered in the inner-most coffin of the tomb of Tutankhamun. It now lies in the Egyptian Museum, Cairo.

Egyptians who rejected Akhenaten's faith erased Tutankhamun's name, along with those of his family, from the records. Tutankhamun might very easily have been all but forgotten.

The clearing of Tutankhamun tomb

But, as it turned out, "King Tut" was to become the most famous of all Egyptian pharaohs entirely because of his tomb. The tomb itself was actually very small, and was not even finished when Tutankhamun died. It was located west of Thebes in the Valley of the Kings, the burial place of most of the New Kingdom pharaohs. While all the other royal tombs in the valley (as well as the great pyramids of the earlier pharaohs) were robbed of their riches in ancient times, the tomb of Tutankhamun remained undiscovered until the twentieth century.

By 1922 a pair of Englishmen, Howard Carter and George Herbert,

Archaeologist Howard Carter (center) supervises the removal
of artifacts from King Tut's tomb.

the wealthy Lord Carnarvon, had spent six years searching without
success for Tutankhamun's tomb. One morning in early November,
Carter's workmen discovered a flight of steps leading to a sealed doorway that had been undisturbed for more than three thousand years.
After waiting for the arrival of Lord Carnarvon, who was in England at
the time, Carter opened the door and found a narrow, rubble-filled pas-
sage leading down to yet another sealed doorway. Making a small
opening in the upper corner of the plaster, Carter held a candle into the
room. Lord Carnarvon, who was eagerly waiting beside him, asked,
"Can you see anything?" Carter answered, "Yes. Wonderful things."

The outer room of the tomb into which Carter had looked was
filled almost to the ceiling with treasure, including gilded wooden

couches and other furniture, chariots, shrines, statues, vases, and box after box of clothing, weapons, jewelry and other personal items— thousands of objects in all. Photographing, removing, and cataloguing these treasures was a difficult task, but this room and its treasure were only the beginning. Another sealed doorway in the north wall of the room led to the king's burial chamber, which was opened in February of 1923. The king's mummy was housed in a series of three coffins, one inside the other. The innermost coffin was made of solid gold. These coffins were placed inside a pink stone sarcophagus and enclosing the sarcophagus were three gilded wooden shrines. Over the head of the mummy was a beautiful and lifelike golden mask.

A New Discovery: The Tomb of Ramesses's Sons

Spectacular finds continue to be made in Egypt today, some-times in locations where previous scholars have already looked. Just such a discovery was recently made in tomb number KV 5 in the Valley of the Kings. The entrance to the tomb was discovered near-ly two hundred years ago, and the outermost rooms were visited by several Egyptologists (including Carter and Lord Carnarvon), none of whom had any idea of the total size of the tomb. The entrance eventually filled with sand, and for more than fifty years its location was lost.

Tomb KV 5 dates to the time of the nineteenth-dynasty pharaoh Ramesses II, whose 66-year reign (from 1290 to 1224 B.C.) was one of the longest in Egyptian history. Ramesses has left more preserved temples and monuments than any other Egyptian king, along with inscriptions describing his military victories in terms that are anything but modest, even for an Egyptian pharaoh. In addition to being an

New Kingdom pharaohs like Tutankhamun began carving their tombs in the rock cliffs west of Thebes, in a valley that is known today as the Valley of the Kings. Tut's tomb lies in the foreground of this picture.

energetic soldier and builder, Ramesses was the father of a huge number of children, including more than fifty sons. He designed KV 5 to be the final resting place for many of these sons.

Egyptologist Kent Weeks, director of the American University in Cairo's Theban Mapping Project, rediscovered the tomb near a parking lot for tourist buses in January 1987. Inside the entrance was a very large hall with sixteen pillars and several smaller rooms off to the sides. A long corridor led off from the back of the large hall. The entire tomb was filled with mud that had been carried into the tomb by floods. Careful excavation will take years.

Early in 1995 Weeks and his team removed a section of ceiling that had collapsed into the long corridor. They were expecting to find a small chamber at the end of the hallway. Instead, they found an elaborate complex of dozens of chambers with carved and painted decorations. Robbers had plundered the tomb in ancient times, but on the floor were the remains of burial offerings, jewelry, pottery, furniture, coffins, and mummified human bodies that the robbers had left behind. In the corridor itself was a beautifully carved and painted statue of the god of the dead, Osiris. The tomb is the largest ever found in Egypt, and its plan is unlike anything known before. Since excavation of the tomb continues today, there is still much more to be learned.

Part Three:
Excavate Your Own Egyptian Artifacts

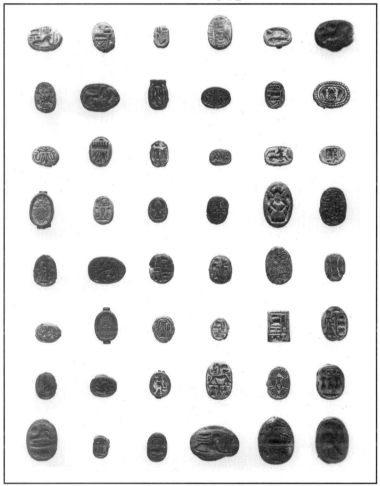

Scarabs

Scarabs and Amulets

An amulet is a small figure worn like a piece of jewelry or placed within the wrappings of a mummy for good luck. The Egyptians used many types of amulets made from a variety of materials. Among the more common amulets were miniature figures of gods, animals, and special hieroglyphic symbols. One of the most popular was the udjat-eye, which was meant to represent the eye of the god Horus. Cut out by Seth, Horus's eye was magically restored and came to be associated with light. The Egyptians wore udjat-eye amulets to protect themselves from evil.

Although the udjat-eye was a common amulet, the scarab [SCARE-rub] was the most popular. A type of beetle that lives in Egypt, the scarab was associated with creation and the sun-god, Ra. The ancient Egyptians believed the scarab to be one of the forms in which Ra appeared on Earth. Because of this, scarabs were thought sacred and were replicated as amulets worn by both the living and the dead. The top of a scarab amulet was shaped like a beetle and the bottom was flat. The flat bottoms were often inscribed with the name of the owner or with other texts and symbols. A special type of scarab, known as a heart scarab, was placed inside mummy wrappings, right over the heart of the deceased. These large scarabs were inscribed with spells designed to protect the heart.

Ushabtis

The Egyptians believed that they would have to do chores for Osiris in the afterlife. Therefore, beginning in the Middle Kingdom, they buried small magical figurines called ushabtis [you-SHOB-tees] which could act as magical substitutes and do the work for them. The earliest ushabtis were simple figures made of wood or wax and shaped like mummies. In the New Kingdom the ushabtis became more elaborate and were made of wood, stone, or a type of glazed earthenware called faience. They were shaped like mummies and were inscribed with the name of the dead person and spells to ensure that they would work effectively. Since their chores involved mainly farm work, the ushabtis sometimes carried tools, such as hoes and baskets.

EXCAVATE AND RESTORE YOUR ARTIFACTS

Now you can excavate your own Egyptian udjat-eye, scarab, and ushabti, just like Egyptologists have done in tombs throughout Egypt for centuries!

ABOVE LEFT: A ushabti figurine. ABOVE RIGHT: Your sand paper, paint tablet, paint brush, excavation tool, and clay block.

In this kit you should have:

- a rectangular slab of rock containing three Egyptian artifacts—an udjat-eye amulet (one part), a ushabti (two parts), and a scarab (two parts).

- a wooden excavation tool

- sandpaper

- a green paint tablet

- a small paintbrush

You will also need:

- some newspaper or a plastic bag to cover your work surface

- a bucket or container of water

- a soft brush, such as an old toothbrush or paintbrush

- paper towels

- brown shoe polish

Excavating Your Artifacts

Excavating your artifacts will take time—allow yourself at least an hour, as this can be very messy if you're not careful. You'll want to work outdoors or indoors on an easy-to-clean surface. Remember to cover your workspace with newspaper or a plastic bag.

1) Place the slab of rock in the container of water and let it soak for at least five minutes. Remove it from the water

and pat it dry with a paper towel. Do not dump out the water yet.

2) Using the wooden excavation tool, scrape away the loose clay to remove your artifacts. Be careful, as ancient artifacts are delicate and can break. If the clay is difficult to remove, you may need to soak the block for a few more minutes.

3) Once the objects are uncovered (there should be five pieces in all), rinse them in water and carefully remove any remaining clay with your brush. When the artifacts are completely clean, lay them out on a paper towel to dry. (If you want to speed up the drying process, use a hair dryer.) Pour the remaining water into a disposable container to discard; do not pour it down the drain.

Restoring Your Artifacts

Many ancient artifacts need to be restored once they have been excavated by archaeologists in the field. Now that you've uncovered your artifacts, you're ready to reconstruct the pieces you've found.

Restoring Your Ushabti

1) Your ushabti should be in two pieces. Use white glue to glue these pieces together. If there are remaining cracks in the statue, scrape

some material from the back of the figure and mix it with a small amount of the glue. You can use this mixture to fill in the cracks.

2) Rub the piece of sandpaper along the back of the statue to remove any unevenness. You should also round any sharp edges.

3) Once the edges are rounded, it's time to paint the statue. Dip your brush in some water and run it across the paint tablet provided. Paint the back of the statue first, making sure that the color is not too dark or too light. Moisten the bristles of the brush only slightly and move them horizontally across the ushabti. Apply water color carefully on the front of the statue, making sure not to let the color seep into the carved hieroglyphs. If some paint does get into the carved cavities, you can scrape it out with a sharp needle or toothpick.

4) Let the paint dry thoroughly. Then, gently apply some brown shoe polish with a soft cloth. Let it dry. Finally, polish with a soft cloth. Your ushabti is now perfect for display in your own ancient Egypt exhibition!

Restoring Your Scarab

1) Check to make sure that the two pieces of the scarab fit together evenly. If not, use the grinding paper to even the fit. Glue the two

flat sides together with white glue.

2) Paint as above, being careful not to let the color seep into the hieroglyphs. Make sure the color isn't too dark or too light.

3) Apply a small amount of polish and finish as above.

Scarabs with carved symbols or texts on their flat sides were often used as seals to mark people's possessions and seal papyrus rolls and containers. Your scarab can be used in the same way. Simply take a small amount of soft clay or wax (the Egyptians even used mud). Make a ball and press it flat with the scarab to leave your mark on the world!

Restoring Your Udjat-eye

1) Clear any excess clay from the center of the eye with a sharp needle or toothpick.

2) Paint as above.

3) Apply polish and finish.

Your amulet is ready to wear! The ancient Egyptians often wore amulets as parts of necklaces and other pieces of jewelry. Cut a piece of string or yarn and thread it through the eye of your amulet. Then, wear it around your neck or wrist. If you have other types of beads, you can string them together with your udjat-eye.

Part Four:
Life in a New Kingdom City—Thebes

The Pharaoh and His Palace

The pharaoh held a unique place in Egyptian society. In spite of being a mortal human, he (or occasionally she) held an office believed to be divine and was therefore treated in many respects like a god. He was regularly called the son of a god (in particular the sun god, Ra), or a "great god" himself. In theory, the pharaoh had control over everything in Egypt and was therefore responsible for its well-being.

The word pharaoh comes from the ancient Egyptian term *per-aa*, meaning "great house," a reference to the palace. The New Kingdom city of Thebes had many palaces, serving a number of different functions. The residential palace was where the pharaoh and his family actually lived. The administrative palace was where most of the official government business took place. Ceremonial palaces were located alongside temples and served a ritual purpose. Funerary palaces were attached to the pharaohs' funerary temples, and were intended to be symbolic homes for the king in eternity. Unfortunately, few royal palaces have been preserved and excavated. The main administrative palace has never been clearly identified, but may have stood near the

This model of Ramesses II's son Merneptah's palace throne room shows the murals that covered the walls, ceilings, and floors of many New Kingdom palaces.

great temple at Karnak. The 18th-dynasty king Amenhotep III built a magnificent residential palace, complete with a manmade lake, in the western part of Thebes at a site called Malkata. Excavations have shown that this palace, built of mud-brick, was decorated with elaborate painted decorations and included its own series of temples and religious buildings.

The great temple at Karnak

The Temple: A Visit to Karnak

The temple complex at Karnak, dedicated to the god Amun, was located in the northern part of the city of Thebes. Rather than a single temple, it is a vast collection of buildings and other monuments built over a period of two thousand years, beginning in the Middle Kingdom. During the New Kingdom, the temple of Amun became the most important temple in all of Egypt.

Surrounding the temple of Amun was a high mud-brick wall. Like all Egyptian temples, the main entrance was marked by a huge, flat stone gateway known today as a *pylon*. Karnak actually has a series of seven pylons, because the temple was enlarged many times. Typically, the pylons were decorated with pictures of the pharaoh defeating his enemies. One of the most impressive parts of the temple at Karnak was the *hypostyle hall,* a roofed space filled with 134 gigantic columns. The actual sanctuary was located farther back in the temple. Most visitors would not have been allowed to enter the interior parts of the temple, and all public festivals would have taken place outside. Numerous festivals were celebrated at the temple of Amun, the most important being *Opet,* which included a colorful procession in which a sacred statue of Amun was carried out in a boat surrounded by priests and other celebrants.

Scribes and Writing

The business of running Egypt's government, as well as all its temples and estates, took a lot of organization, and during the New Kingdom Thebes would have housed a large number of scribes for this purpose. Most of the people in ancient Egypt could not read or write, so scribes were trained to read and write the hieroglyphic script. Egyptians would hire a scribe whenever they wanted to write a letter or read letters they had received. Scribes were a very highly respected class of people. Not only were they in great demand, but they were the only people with first-hand news about what was going on in the government. From the writings they left behind, it seems that scribes were well aware of their own importance and sometimes viewed other occupations with disdain.

Writing developed in Egypt around 3100 B.C. For most of their history, the Egyptians wrote with signs known today as *hieroglyphs* [HIGH-row-gliffs]. The earliest hieroglyphs probably represented actual things or ideas. Very quickly, however, hieroglyphs came to represent sounds, so that a series of hiero-

An Egyptian scribe at work

glyphs could be used to spell a word. Therefore, while some single hieroglyphic signs do represent a whole word, others function in much the same way as our own letters of the alphabet. One major difference between the Egyptian writing system and our own is that the Egyptians did not write any vowels. Since all we have are the consonants, it is difficult to know how many of the words really sounded.

The Village at Deir el Medineh: A Day in the Life

Neferhotep and Baket lived with their family in the workers' village known today by its modern name, Deir el Medineh [Deer el med-EE-na]. Not far away, along the Nile river, was the bustling city of Thebes, with its massive temples and palaces, docks and storehouses, and crowded streets lined with mudbrick houses. To the villagers of Deir el Medineh, Thebes was known simply as "the city." The town in which Neferhotep and Baket lived was located in the desert, at the foot of the limestone cliffs to the west of Thebes near the royal cemeteries. It was the home of the people responsible for cutting, decorating, and supplying the royal tombs. As such, it was unique among Egyptian villages. While most Egyptians were farmers, the people of Deir el Medineh were expert craftsmen, stonemasons, artists, and scribes.

Like most of the village houses, Baket and Neferhotep's home consisted of only a few rooms, with stairs leading up to the roof. Much activity took place on the roof, and the family often slept there during the summer. The main room, supported by a wooden column, was furnished with cushioned chairs and couches. It also housed the family shrine, which included a small stone slab, or *stela*, mounted on the wall and the busts of their ancestors. The kitchen was at the back of the house, and it was here that Baket helped her mother and the other women of the house to grind flour, bake bread, and brew beer. Since Deir el Medineh was located in the desert, nearly all food products, as well as water for cooking and drinking, were shipped in from Thebes.

Because they were relatively well-off, Baket's family was able to maintain servants on a part-time basis to help them with the work. As the "mistress of the house," her mother, Henut, oversaw the daily activities of both the servants and the other women of the household.

Neferhotep was training to be a scribe like his father, Paneb, who had the important responsibility of keeping the accounts for one of the two groups of men at work on the royal tomb. He attended a special scribal school, where his tools included a wooden palette with containers for red and black paint and a slot for storing brushes. The brushes themselves were made of reeds, and when Neferhotep ran short he prepared more by carefully chewing the ends off fresh reeds. To carry his equipment, he wrapped it in a small bundle tied with a string. Although papyrus had been in use for centuries, Neferhotep practiced his writing on flat flakes of limestone. The cutting of tombs created vast amounts of flaked limestone, making it an easily available material for students to use for practice lessons.

Learning to be a scribe was not easy, and Neferhotep's teacher, his uncle Ramose, believed in strict discipline. Like other Egyptian students, Neferhotep spent long hours copying and memorizing texts that were often hundreds of years old. The moral instructions, a class of texts that provided lists of rules and bits of advice, were the most commonly used texts for these tasks. Ramose was fond of giving such advice himself, and often reminded his nephew that being a scribe was far better than working in any other profession. When Neferhotep failed to pay attention to these instructions or seemed to be distracted from his lessons, his teacher, like many Egyptian scribal instructors, might well resort to beating him with a reed. Neferhotep could look forward to many more years of education; he would continue to study with a senior scribe well after his basic schooling was complete, even while he began serving in the local administration as a young man.

Feast days provided a welcome break from routine for Baket, Neferhotep, and their family. Food from the storerooms was brought out in large quantities and a feast was prepared. The entire household

visited the family's shrine and tomb chapel in order to share the food and drink with their dead ancestors. On such holidays, Baket would set aside a loaf of her favorite honey cake from the kitchen to offer in honor of her grandmother Baket, after whom she had been named.

At the village temples, Baket and Neferhotep's parents made offerings to the local Theban gods, as well as to dead pharaohs. On some occasions, a statue of the 18th-dynasty king Amenhotep I, who founded the village and was revered as a god, was carried out of his shrine. The villagers asked questions and presented their problems to the dead king in the hopes that he would answer and advise them through his sacred image. Sometimes, the procession would stop and the statue would seem to look out or nod in response to a question. For Neferhotep and Baket, the image inspired great awe and excitement.

Activity: *Writing in Hieroglyphs*

Here are some of the hieroglyphs that have alphabetic sound values. (Note that in order to make it easier, some signs have been adapted to serve as vowels.) The direction of hieroglyphic writing varied, but they were usually written from left to right, just like English. When written horizontally, the symbols should face the beginning of the line of text.

Try your hand at your own name; then try to compose sentences. Send secret messages to your friends!

A (vulture)	
B (foot)	
C [like "k"] (basket)	
C [like "s"] (folded cloth)	
D (hand)	
E (arm)	
F (viper)	
G (stand for jar)	
H (hut)	
I (reed leaf)	
J (snake)	
K (basket)	
L (lion)	

M (owl)	
N (waves of water)	
O (vulture)	
P (stool)	
Q (hillside)	
R (mouth)	
S (folded cloth)	
Sh (pool)	
T (bread loaf)	
U (quail chick)	
V (viper)	
W (quail chick)	
X (basket and folded cloth)	
Y (two reed leaves)	
Z (bolt)	

Part Five:
The Egyptians and Their Influence Today

Modern Cairo

Although the ancient Egyptians lived many centuries ago, their culture continues to influence people today. Modern Egyptians living in the Nile valley still use methods of irrigation invented by the ancient Egyptians thousands of years earlier. While Egyptians speak Arabic today, a version of the ancient language is still used in Egypt's Christian churches. The Egyptian Christians are called *Copts* and the language is called *Coptic*.

The Egyptians were among the first people to use many of the materials we take for granted today, such as linen, paper, and glass. Many foods and beverages enjoyed today were also developed by the Egyptians. The Greeks learned brewing from the ancient Egyptians, and malt beverages have been produced in Europe ever since. The ancient Egyptians have also been credited with the domestication of the cat.

The art and architecture of Egypt influenced many other ancient peoples such as the Greeks, who modeled some of their earliest large scale stone sculptures after Egyptian statues. Some columns and other elements were also borrowed from the Egyptians. But it is not only ancient people who draw from Egyptian models. In the twentieth century, architects still use ideas devised from the Egyptians. In fact, one of the best-known structures in the United States, the Washington Monument, is a copy of an Egyptian obelisk, a type of monument found at temples like Karnak.

The legacy of the ancient Egyptians lives on. Almost anywhere we look we can find traces of their

The cat, along with many other animals, was linked to Egyptian gods.
Figures of cats, like this 600 B.C. statuette, were common.

The Washington Monument is one of many modern structures
drawn from Egyptian models.

civilization, and the more we learn about them, the more we understand the world around us. If you visit Egypt today you will be surrounded by the achievements of these magnificent people. Look closely at the monuments around you. You may find the entrance to a hidden tomb!

About the Author

D r. *Denise Doxey* is a researcher in the Egyptian section of the University of Pennsylvania Museum of Archaeology and Anthropology and a lecturer for the University's Department of Asian and Middle Eastern Studies, where she teaches courses in the language and literature of ancient Egypt. Dr. Doxey has excavated sites in Egypt and Greece and has written on ancient Egyptian culture and society. She lives in Philadelphia with her husband, Paul Giblin, two cats, a dog, and a parrot.